# The Key Facts™ on

# Nepal

*Essential Information on Nepal*

By Patrick W. Nee

The Internationalist®

www.internationalist.com

**The Internationalist**®

*International Business, Investment, and Travel*

**Published by:**

The Internationalist Publishing Company

96 Walter Street/ Suite 200

Boston, MA 02131, USA

Tel: 617-354-7722

www.internationalist.com

PN@internationalist.com

# *Table Of Contents*

# Chapter 1: Background

In 1951, the Nepali monarch ended the century-old system of rule by hereditary premiers and instituted a cabinet system of government. Reforms in 1990 established a multiparty democracy within the framework of a constitutional monarchy. An insurgency led by Maoists broke out in 1996. The ensuing 10-year civil war between Maoist and government forces witnessed the dissolution of the cabinet and parliament and assumption of absolute power by the king in 2002. Several weeks of mass protests in April 2006 were followed by several months of peace negotiations between the Maoists and government officials, and culminated in a late 2006 peace accord and the promulgation of an interim constitution. Following a nationwide election in April 2008, the newly formed Constituent Assembly (CA) declared Nepal a federal democratic republic and abolished the monarchy at its first meeting the following month. The CA elected the country's first president in July. Between 2008 and 2011 there were four different coalition governments, led twice by the United Communist Party of Nepal-Maoist, which received a plurality of votes in the 2008 CA election, and twice by the Communist Party of Nepal-United Marxist-Leninist (UML). After the CA failed to draft a constitution by the May 2012 deadline set by the Supreme Court, then

Prime Minister Baburam BHATTARAI dissolved the CA. Months of negotiations ensued until March 2013 when the major political parties agreed to create an interim government headed by then Chief Justice Khil Raj REGMI with a mandate to hold elections for a new CA. Elections were held in November 2013, in which and the Nepali Congress won the largest share of the seats in the CA and in February 2014 formed a coalition government with the second place UML and with Nepali Congress President Sushil KOIRALA as prime minister

# Chapter 2: Geography

**Location:**

Southern Asia, between China and India

**Geographic coordinates:**

28 00 N, 84 00 E

**Map references:**

Asia

**Area:**

total: 147,181 sq km

country comparison to the world: 94

land: 143,351 sq km

water: 3,830 sq km

**Area - comparative:**

slightly larger than Arkansas

**Land boundaries:**

total: 2,926 km

border countries: China 1,236 km, India 1,690 km

**Coastline:**

0 km (landlocked)

**Maritime claims:**

none (landlocked)

**Climate:**

varies from cool summers and severe winters in north to subtropical summers and mild winters in south

**Terrain:**

Tarai or flat river plain of the Ganges in south, central hill region, rugged Himalayas in north

**Elevation extremes:**

lowest point: Kanchan Kalan 70 m

highest point: Mount Everest 8,850 m (highest point in Asia)

**Natural resources:**

quartz, water, timber, hydropower, scenic beauty, small deposits of lignite, copper, cobalt, iron ore

**Land use:**

arable land: 16%

permanent crops: 0.8%

other: 83.2% (2011)

**Irrigated land:**

11,680 sq km (2003)

**Total renewable water resources:**

210.2 cu km (2011)

**Freshwater withdrawal (domestic/industrial/agricultural):**

total: 9.5 cu km/yr (2%/0%/98%)

per capita: 334.7 cu m/yr (2006)

**Natural hazards:**

severe thunderstorms; flooding; landslides; drought and famine depending on the timing, intensity, and duration of the summer monsoons

**Environment - current issues:**

deforestation (overuse of wood for fuel and lack of alternatives); contaminated water (with human and animal wastes, agricultural runoff, and industrial effluents); wildlife conservation; vehicular emissions

**Environment - international agreements:**

party to: Biodiversity, Climate Change, Climate Change-Kyoto Protocol, Desertification, Endangered Species, Hazardous Wastes, Law of the Sea, Ozone Layer Protection, Tropical Timber 83, Tropical Timber 94, Wetlands

signed, but not ratified: Marine Life Conservation

**Geography - note:**

landlocked; strategic location between China and India; contains eight of world's 10 highest peaks, including Mount Everest and Kanchenjunga - the world's tallest and third tallest - on the borders with China and India respectively

# Chapter 3: People and Society

**Nationality:**

noun: Nepali (singular and plural)

adjective: Nepali

**Ethnic groups:**

Chhettri 16.6%, Brahman-Hill 12.2%, Magar 7.1%, Tharu 6.6%, Tamang 5.8%, Newar 5%, Kami 4.8%, Muslim 4.4%, Yadav 4%, Rai 2.3%, Gurung 2%, Damai/Dholii 1.8%, Thakuri 1.6%, Limbu 1.5%, Sarki 1.4%, Teli 1.4%, Chamar/Harijan/Ram 1.3%, Koiri/Kushwaha 1.2%, other 23%

note: 125 caste/ethnic groups were reported in the 2011 national census (2011 est.)

**Languages:**

Khmer (official) 96.3%, other 3.7% (2008 est.) Nepali (official) 44.6%, Maithali 11.7%, Bhojpuri 6%, Tharu 5.8%, Tamang 5.1%, Newar 3.2%, Magar 3%, Bajjika 3%, Urdu 2.6%, Avadhi 1.9%, Limbu 1.3%, Gurung 1.2%, other 10.4%, unspecified 0.2%

note: 123 languages reported as mother tongue in 2011 national census; many in government and business also speak English (2011 est.)

**Religions:**

Hindu 81.3%, Buddhist 9%, Muslim 4.4%, Kirant 3%, Christian 1.4%, other 0.5%, unspecifed 0.2% (2011 est.)

**Population:**

> 30,986,975 (July 2014 est.)
>
> country comparison to the world: 42

**Age structure:**

> 0-14 years: 31.6% (male 4,989,268/female 4,805,381)
>
> 15-24 years: 22.6% (male 3,521,421/female 3,484,203)
>
> 25-54 years: 35.7% (male 5,273,079/female 5,775,404)
>
> 55-64 years: 4.5% (male 847,431/female 886,760)
>
> 65 years and over: 4.5% (male 648,917/female 755,111)
>
> (2014 est.)

**Dependency ratios:**

> total dependency ratio: 66.1 %
>
> youth dependency ratio: 57.6 %
>
> elderly dependency ratio: 8.5 %
>
> potential support ratio: 11.7 (2013)

**Median age:**

> total: 22.9 years
>
> male: 22.2 years
>
> female: 23.6 years (2014 est.)

**Population growth rate:**

> 1.82% (2014 est.)
>
> country comparison to the world: 66

**Birth rate:**

> 21.07 births/1,000 population (2014 est.)
>
> country comparison to the world: 79

**Death rate:**

6.62 deaths/1,000 population (2014 est.)

country comparison to the world: 145

**Net migration rate:**

3.71 migrant(s)/1,000 population (2014 est.)

country comparison to the world: 32

**Urbanization:**

urban population: 17% of total population (2011)

rate of urbanization: 3.62% annual rate of change (2010-15 est.)

**Major urban areas - population:**

KATHMANDU (capital) 990,000 (2009)

**Sex ratio:**

at birth: 1.04 male(s)/female

0-14 years: 1.04 male(s)/female

15-24 years: 1.01 male(s)/female

25-54 years: 0.91 male(s)/female

55-64 years: 0.97 male(s)/female

65 years and over: 0.87 male(s)/female

total population: 0.96 male(s)/female (2014 est.)

**Mother's mean age at first birth:**

20.1

notemedian age at first birth among women 25-29 (2011 est.)

**Maternal mortality rate:**

170 deaths/100,000 live births (2010)

country comparison to the world: 60

**Infant mortality rate:**

total: 40.43 deaths/1,000 live births

country comparison to the world: 53

male: 40.5 deaths/1,000 live births

female: 40.35 deaths/1,000 live births (2014 est.)

**Life expectancy at birth:**

total population: 67.19 years

country comparison to the world: 165

male: 65.88 years

female: 68.56 years (2014 est.)

**Total fertility rate:**

2.3 children born/woman (2014 est.)

country comparison to the world: 93

**Contraceptive prevalence rate:**

49.7% (2011)

**Health expenditures:**

5.4% of GDP (2011)

country comparison to the world: 126

**Physicians density:**

0.21 physicians/1,000 population (2004)

**Hospital bed density:**

4.7 beds/1,000 population (2009)

**Drinking water source:**

improved:

*urban*: 91.2% of population

*rural*: 86.8% of population

*total*: 87.6% of population

unimproved:

*urban*: 8.8% of population

*rural*: 13.2% of population

*total*: 12.4% of population (2011 est.)

**Sanitation facility access:**

improved:

*urban*: 50.1% of population

*rural*: 32.4% of population

*total*: 35.4% of population

unimproved:

*urban*: 49.9% of population

*rural*: 67.6% of population

*total*: 64.6% of population (2011 est.)

**HIV/AIDS - adult prevalence rate:**

0.3% (2012 est.)

country comparison to the world: 99

**HIV/AIDS - people living with HIV/AIDS:**

48,700 (2012 est.)

country comparison to the world: 61

**HIV/AIDS - deaths:**

4,100 (2012 est.)

country comparison to the world: 44

**Major infectious diseases:**

degree of risk: high

food or waterborne diseases: bacterial diarrhea, hepatitis A and E, and typhoid fever

vectorborne diseases: Japanese encephalitis, malaria, and dengue fever (2013)

**Obesity - adult prevalence rate:**

1.4% (2008)

country comparison to the world: 189

**Children under the age of 5 underweight:**

29.1% (2011)

country comparison to the world: 18

**Education expenditures:**

4.7% of GDP (2010)

country comparison to the world: 87

**Literacy:**

definition: age 15 and over can read and write

total population: 57.4%

male: 71.1%

female: 46.7% (2011 est.)

**School life expectancy (primary to tertiary education):**

> total: 12 years

> male: 12 years

> female: 13 years (2011)

**Child labor – children ages 5-14:**

> total number: 2,467,549

> percentage: 34 % (2008 est.)

# Chapter 4: Government and Key Leaders

**Country name:**

> <u>conventional long form</u>: Federal Democratic Republic of
> Nepal
>
> <u>conventional short form</u>: Nepal
>
> <u>local long form</u>: Sanghiya Loktantrik Ganatantra Nepal
>
> <u>local short form</u>: Nepal

**Government type:**

> federal democratic republic

**Capital:**

> <u>name</u>: Kathmandu
>
> <u>geographic coordinates</u>: 27 43 N, 85 19 E
>
> <u>time difference</u>: UTC+5.75 (10.75 hours ahead of
> Washington, DC during Standard Time)

**Administrative divisions:**

> 14 zones (anchal, singular and plural); Bagmati, Bheri,
> Dhawalagiri, Gandaki, Janakpur, Karnali, Kosi, Lumbini,
> Mahakali, Mechi, Narayani, Rapti, Sagarmatha, Seti

**Independence:**

> 1768 (unified by Prithvi Narayan SHAH)

**National holiday:**

> Republic Day, 29 May

**Constitution:**

several previous; latest entered into force 15 January 2007 (interim); note -a Constituent Assembly (CA) elected in 2008 to draft and promulgate a new constitution was unsuccessful and was disolved in mid-2012; a new CA was elected in late 2013 and the parties have committed to promulgating a new constitution within one year of the CAs first sitting of January 2014 (2013)

**Legal system:**

English common law and Hindu legal concepts

**International law organization participation:**

has not submitted an ICJ jurisdiction declaration; non-party state to the ICCt

**Suffrage:**

18 years of age; universal

**Executive branch:**

chief of state: President Ram Baran YADAV (since 23 July 2008); Vice President Paramananda JHA (since 23 July 2008)

head of government: Prime Minister Sushil KOIRALA (since 11 February 2014)

cabinet: Prime Minister Koirala on 25 February 2014 appointed the cabinet ministers; the cabinet is dominated by the Nepali Congress and the Communist Party of Nepal-United Marxist-Leninist elections: president elected by Parliament; term extends until the new constitution is promulgated; president elected on 21 July 2008; date of next election NA

election results: Ram Baran YADAV elected president by the Constituent Assembly in a second round of voting on 21 July 2008; Ram Baran YADAV 308, Ram Jaja Prasad SINGH 282

**Legislative branch:**

unicameral Constituent Assembly (601 seats; 240 members elected by direct popular vote, 335 by proportional representation, and 26 appointed by the Cabinet (Council of Ministers); note - interim government Chairman REGMI convened Nepal's second Constituency Assembly on 22 January 2014

elections: last held on 19 November 2013 (next to be held NA)

election results: percent of vote by party - NC 26%, CPN-UML 24%, Unified Communist Party of Nepal (Maoist) 15%, Rastriya Prajatantra Party Nepal 7%; other 26%; seats by party - NC 196, CPN-UML 175, UCPN(M) 80, Rastriya Prajantantra Party Nepal 24, other smaller parties 100; note - 26 seats filled by the new Cabinet have not yet been appointed

**Judicial branch:**

Highest court(s): Supreme Court (consists of the chief justice and up to 14 judges

note: note - Nepal's judiciary was restructured under its 2007 Interim Constitution

Judge selection and term of offfice: the Supreme Court chief justice appointed by the prime minister on the recommendation of the Constitutional Council; other judges are appointed by the prime minister on the recommendation of the Judicial Council; judges serve until age 65

subordinate courts: appellate and district courts

**Political parties and leaders:**

note: 120 political parties participated in the 19 November 2013 election and the 30 parties listed below were elected to serve in the Constituent Assembly

Akhanda Nepal Party [Kumar KHADKA]

Communist Party of Nepal-Marxist Leninist [C.P. MAINALI]

Communist Party of Nepal-Unified Marxist-Leninist or UML [Jhalanath KHANAL]

Communist Party of Nepal (United) [Chandra Dev JOSHI]

Dalit Janajati Party [Bishwendra PASHWAN]

Federal Socialist Party [Ashok RAI]

Jana Jagaran Party Nepal [Lok Mani DHAKAL]

Khambuwan Rastriya Morcha-Nepal [Ram Kumar RAI]

Madhesi People's Rights Forum-Democratic [Bijay Kumar GACHCHADAR]

Madhesi People's Rights Forum-Nepal [Upendra YADAV]

Madhesi People's Rights Forum-Republican [Raj Kishore YADAV]

Madhes Samata Party Nepal [Meghraj SAHANI]

National Madhes Socialist Party [Sharat Singh BHANDARI]

Nepal Pariwar Dal [Ek Nath DHAKAL]

Nepal Workers and Peasants Party [Narayan Man BIJUKCHHE]

Nepali Congress [Sushil KOIRALA]

Nepali Janata Dal [Hari Charan SAH]

Nepa Rastriya Party [Keshav Man SHAKYA]

Rastriya Janamorcha Nepal [Chitra Bahadur K.C.]

Rastriya Janamukti Party [Malwar Singh THAPA]

Rastriya Prajatantra Party [Surya Bahadur THAPA]

Rastriya Prajatantra Party-Nepal [Kamal THAPA]

Sadbhavana Party [Rajendra MAHATO]

Samajbadi Janata Party Nepal [Prem Bahadur SINGH]

Sanghiya Sadbhavana Party [Anil JHA]

Sanghiye Lokatantrik Rastriya Manch [Rukmini CHAUDARY]

Terai Madhes Democratic Party [Mahantha THAKUR]

Terai Madhes Sadbhavana Party-Nepal [Mahendra YADAV]

Tharuhat Terai Party Nepal [Bhanuram CHAUDARY]

Unified Communist Party of Nepal (Maoist) or UCPN(M) [Pushpa Kamal DAHAL, also known as PRACHANDA]

**Political pressure groups and leaders:**

The Communist Party of Nepal - Maoist (CPN-M); note - this party split from the UCPN(M) in June 2012,opposed the November 2013 elections, and is not represented in the current Constituent Assembly

other: a variety of groups advocating regional autonomy such as the Federal State Limbuwan Council in far eastern Nepal

**International organization participation:**

ADB, BIMSTEC, CD, CP, FAO, G-77, IAEA, IBRD, ICAO, ICC, ICRM, IDA, IFAD, IFC, IFRCS, ILO, IMF, IMO, Interpol, IOC, IOM, IPU, ISO (correspondent), ITSO, ITU, ITUC (NGOs), MIGA, MINURSO, MINUSMA, MINUSTAH, MONUSCO, NAM, OPCW, SAARC, SACEP, UN, UNAMID, UNCTAD, UNESCO, UNIDO, UNIFIL, UNISFA, UNMIL, UNMISS, UNMIT, UNOCI, UNTSO, UNWTO, UPU, WCO, WFTU (NGOs), WHO, WIPO, WMO, WTO

**Diplomatic representation in the US:**

chief of mission: ambassador (vacant); Chargé d'Affaires Rishi Ram GHIMIRE (since 22 January 2014) chancery: 2131 Leroy Place NW, Washington, DC 20008

telephone: [1] (202) 667-4550

FAX: [1] (202) 667-5534

consulate(s) general: New York

**Diplomatic representation from the US:**

chief of mission: Ambassador Peter W. BODDE (since 21 September 2012)

embassy: Maharajgunj, Kathmandu

mailing address: use embassy street address

telephone: [977] (1) 423-4000

FAX: [977] (1) 400-7272

**Key Leaders:**

| | |
|---|---|
| Pres. | Ram Baran YADAV, *Dr.* |
| Vice Pres. | Paramananda JHA |
| Chmn., Interim Council of Ministers for Elections | Khil Raj REGMI |
| Min. for Agricultural Development | Tek Bahadur Thapa GHARTI |
| Min. of Commerce & Supplies | Shanker Prasad KOIRALA |
| Min. of Constituent Assembly Affairs | Hari Prasad NEUPANE |
| Min. of Culture | Ram Kumar SHRESTHA |
| Min. of Defense | Khil Raj REGMI |
| Min. of Education | Madhav Prasad PAUDEL |
| Min. of Energy | Uma Kanta JHA |
| Min. of Environment | Uma Kanta JHA |
| Min. of Federal Affairs | Bidhyadhar MALLIK |
| Min. of Finance | Shanker Prasad KOIRALA |
| Min. of Foreign Affairs | Madhav Prasad GHIMIRE |
| Min. of Forest & Soil Conservation | Tek Bahadur Thapa GHARTI |
| Min. of Gen. Admin. | Madhav Prasad PAUDEL |

| | |
|---|---|
| Min. of Health & Population | Bidhyadhar MALLIK |
| Min. of Home Affairs | Madhav Prasad GHIMIRE |
| Min. of Industry | Shanker Prasad KOIRALA |
| Min. of Information & Communications | Madhav Prasad PAUDEL |
| Min. of Irrigation | Uma Kanta JHA |
| Min. of Labor & Employment | Hari Prasad NEUPANE |
| Min. of Land Reforms & Management | Ridhi Baba PRADHAN |
| Min. of Law & Justice | Hari Prasad NEUPANE |
| Min. of Local Development | Bidhyadhar MALLIK |
| Min. of Parliamentary Affairs | Hari Prasad NEUPANE |
| Min. of Peace & Reconstruction | Ram Kumar SHRESTHA |
| Min. for Physical Infrastructure & Transportation | Chhabi Raj PANTA |
| Min. of Science & Technology | Uma Kanta JHA |
| Min. of Tourism & Civil Aviation | Ram Kumar SHRESTHA |
| Min. for Urban Development | Chhabi Raj PANTA |
| Min. of Women, Children, & Social Welfare | Ridhi Baba PRADHAN |
| Min. of Youth & Sports | Ram Kumar SHRESTHA |
| Governor, Central Bank | Yuvraj KHATIWADA |
| Ambassador to the US | Shankar Prasad SHARMA |
| Permanent Representative to the UN, New York | Durga Prasad BHATTARAI |

**Flag description:**

red with a blue border around the unique shape of two overlapping right triangles; the smaller, upper triangle bears a white stylized moon and the larger, lower triangle displays a white 12-pointed sun; the color red represents the rhododendron (Nepal's national flower) and is a sign of victory and bravery, the blue border signifies peace and harmony; the two right triangles are a combination of two single pennons (pennants) that originally symbolized the Himalaya Mountains while their charges represented the families of the king (upper) and the prime minister, but today they are understood to denote Hinduism and Buddhism, the country's two main religions; the moon represents the serenity of the Nepalese people and the shade and cool weather in the Himalayas, while the sun depicts the heat and higher temperatures of the lower parts of Nepal; the moon and the sun are also said to express the hope that the nation will endure as long as these heavenly bodies

note:  Nepal is the only country in the world whose flag is not rectangular or square

**National symbol(s):**

rhododendron blossom

**National anthem:**

name: "Sayaun Thunga Phool Ka" (Hundreds of Flowers)

lyrics/music: CHUON NAT/F. PERRUCHOT and J. JEKYLLPradeep Kumar RAI/Ambar GURUNG

note: adopted 1941, restored 1993; the anthem, based on a Cambodian folk tune, was restored after the defeat of the Communist regime adopted 2007; after the abolition of the monarchy in 2006, a new anthem was required because of the previous anthem's praise for the king

# Chapter 5: Economy

**Economy - overview:**

Nepal is among the poorest and least developed countries in the world, with about one-quarter of its population living below the poverty line. Nepal is heavily dependent on remittances, which amount to as much as 22-25% of GDP. Agriculture is the mainstay of the economy, providing a livelihood for more than 70% of the population and accounting for a little over one-third of GDP. Industrial activity mainly involves the processing of agricultural products, including pulses, jute, sugarcane, tobacco, and grain. Nepal has considerable scope for exploiting its potential in hydropower, with an estimated 42,000 MW of commercially feasible capacity, but political uncertainty and a difficult business climate have hampered foreign investment. Additional challenges to Nepal's growth include its landlocked geographic location, persistent power shortages, underdeveloped transportation infrastructure, civil strife and labor unrest, and its susceptibility to natural disaster. The lack of political consensus in the past several years has delayed national budgets and prevented much-needed economic reform, although the government passed a full budget in 2013.

**GDP (purchasing power parity):**

$42.06 billion (2013 est.)

country comparison to the world: 104

$40.57 billion (2012 est.)

$38.7 billion (2011 est.)

note: data are in 2013 US dollars

**GDP (official exchange rate):**

$19.34 billion (2013 est.)

**GDP - real growth rate:**

3.6% (2013 est.)

country comparison to the world: 89

4.9% (2012 est.)

3.4% (2011 est.)

**GDP - per capita (PPP):**

$1,500 (2013 est.)

country comparison to the world: 205

$1,500 (2012 est.)

$1,400 (2011 est.)

note: data are in 2013 US dollars

**GDP – composition, by end use:**

household consumption: 81.2%

government consumption: 10%

investment in fixed capital: 21.6%

investment in inventories: 14.6%

exports of goods and services: 10.3%

imports of goods and services: -37.7% (2013 est.)

**GDP - composition by sector:**

agriculture: 36.8%

industry: 14.5%

services: 48.7% (2013 est.)

**Agriculture – products:**

pulses, rice, corn, wheat, sugarcane, jute, root crops; milk, water buffalo meat

**Industries:**

tourism, carpets, textiles; small rice, jute, sugar, and oilseed mills; cigarettes, cement and brick production

**Industrial production growth rate:**

1.5% (2013 est.)

country comparison to the world: 137

**Labor force:**

16 million

country comparison to the world: 39

note: severe lack of skilled labor (2011 est.)

**Labor force - by occupation:**

agriculture: 75%

industry: 7%

services: 18% (2010 est.)

**Unemployment rate:**

46% (2008 est.)

country comparison to the world: 193

42% (2004 est.)

**Population below poverty line:**

25.2% (2011 est.)

**Household income or consumption by percentage share:**

lowest 10%: 3.2%

highest 10%: 29.5% (2011)

**Distribution of family income - Gini index:**

32.8 (2010)

country comparison to the world: 102

47.2 (2008 est.)

**Budget:**

revenues: $3.3 billion

expenditures: $3.9 billion (FY12/13)

**Taxes and other revenues:**

17.1% of GDP (FY12/13)

country comparison to the world: 182

**Budget surplus (+) or deficit (-):**

-3.1% of GDP (FY12/13)

country comparison to the world: 126

**Public Debt:**

28% of GDP

country comparison to the world: 126

**Inflation rate (consumer prices):**

9.6% (2013 est.)

country comparison to the world: 207

9.5% (2012 est.)

**Central bank discount rate:**

6% (31 December 2010 est.)

country comparison to the world: 49

6.5% (31 December 2009 est.)

**Commercial bank prime lending rate:**

9% (31 December 2013 est.)

country comparison to the world: 117

8% (31 December 2012 est.)

**Stock of narrow money:**

$3.553 billion (31 December 2013 est.)

country comparison to the world: 114

$3.104 billion (31 December 2012 est.)

**Stock of broad money:**

$11.49 billion (31 December 2013 est.)

country comparison to the world: 100

$11.71 billion (31 December 2012 est.)

**Stock of domestic credit:**

$13.46 billion (31 December 2013 est.)

country comparison to the world: 90

$11.88 billion (31 December 2012 est.)

**Market value of publicly traded shares:**

$4.16 billion (31 December 2012 est.)

country comparison to the world: 90

$3.849 billion (31 December 2011)

$5.235 billion (31 December 2010 est.)

**Current account balance:**

$648 million (2013 est.)

country comparison to the world: 50

$283.9 million (2012 est.)

**Exports:**

$1.06 billion (2013 est.)

country comparison to the world: 156

$1.004 billion (2012 est.)

**Exports - commodities:**

clothing, pulses, carpets, textiles, juice, pashima, jute goods

**Exports - partners:**

India 93.9%, Bangladesh 4%, Italy 0.4% (2013 est.)

**Imports:**

$6.329 billion (2013 est.)

country comparison to the world: 119

$5.951 billion (2012 est.)

**Imports - commodities:**

petroleum products, machinery and equipment, gold, electrical goods, medicine

**Imports - partners:**

UAE 6.2%, South Korea 3.1%, China 2.5% (2013 est.)

**Reserves of foreign exchange and gold:**

$6.574 billion (15 January 2014 est.)

country comparison to the world: 85

$5.833 billion (15 July 2013 est.)

**Debt - external:**

$3.956 billion (31 December 2011 est.)

country comparison to the world: 128

$3.673 billion (31 December 2010 est.)

**Stock of direct foreign investment – at home:**

$103 million

country comparison to the world: 105

**Stock of direct foreign investment – abroad:**

$NA

**Exchange rates:**

Nepalese rupees (NPR) per US dollar -

87.96 (2013 est.)

85.2 (2012 est.)

73.16 (2010 est.)

77.44 (2009)

65.21 (2008)

# Chapter 6: Energy

**Electricity - production:**

>3.431 billion kWh (2012 est.)

>country comparison to the world: 128

**Electricity - consumption:**

>2.745 billion kWh (2010 est.)

>country comparison to the world: 133

**Electricity - exports:**

>30 million kWh (2010 est.)

>country comparison to the world: 86

**Electricity - imports:**

>694 million kWh (2010 est.)

>country comparison to the world: 71

**Electricity - installed generating capacity:**

>721,000 kW (2010 est.)

>country comparison to the world: 129

**Electricity - from fossil fuels:**

>7.9% of total installed capacity (2010 est.)

>country comparison to the world: 198

**Electricity - from nuclear fuels:**

>0% of total installed capacity (2010 est.)

>country comparison to the world: 153

**Electricity - from hydroelectric plants:**

>92.1% of total installed capacity (2010 est.)

>country comparison to the world: 10

**Electricity - from other renewable sources:**

0% of total installed capacity (2010 est.)

country comparison to the world: 107

**Crude oil - production:**

0 bbl/day (2012 est.)

country comparison to the world: 202

**Crude oil - exports:**

0 bbl/day (2010 est.)

country comparison to the world: 163

**Crude oil - imports:**

0 bbl/day (2010 est.)

country comparison to the world: 105

**Crude oil - proved reserves:**

0 bbl (1 January 2013 es)

country comparison to the world: 172

**Refined petroleum products - production:**

0 bbl/day (2010 est.)

country comparison to the world: 182

**Refined petroleum products - consumption:**

18,430 bbl/day (2011 est.)

country comparison to the world: 132

**Refined petroleum products - exports:**

0 bbl/day (2010 est.)

country comparison to the world: 204

**Refined petroleum products - imports:**

21,960 bbl/day (2010 est.)

country comparison to the world: 102

**Natural gas - production:**

0 cu m (2011 est.)

country comparison to the world: 175

**Natural gas - consumption:**

0 cu m (2010 est.)

country comparison to the world: 180

**Natural gas - exports:**

0 cu m (2011 est.)

country comparison to the world: 157

**Natural gas - imports:**

0 cu m (2011 est.)

country comparison to the world: 108

**Natural gas - proved reserves:**

0 cu m (1 January 2013 es)

country comparison to the world: 178

**Carbon dioxide emissions from consumption of energy:**

3.173 million Mt (2011 est.)

country comparison to the world: 139

# Chapter 7: Communications

**Telephones - main lines in use:**

834,000 (2013)

country comparison to the world: 83

**Telephones - mobile cellular:**

18.138 million (2013)

country comparison to the world: 54

**Telephone system:**

general assessment: poor telephone and telegraph service; fair radiotelephone communication service and mobile-cellular telephone network

domestic: mobile-cellular telephone subscribership base is increasing with roughly 90% of the population living in areas covered by mobile carriers

international: country code - 977; radiotelephone communications; microwave and fiber landlines to India; satellite earth station - 1 Intelsat (Indian Ocean) (2011)

**Broadcast media:**

state operates 2 TV stations as well as national and regional radio stations; roughly 30 independent TV channels are registered with only about half in regular operation; nearly 400 FM radio stations are licensed with roughly 300 operational (2007)

**Internet country code:**

.np

**Internet hosts:**

41,256 (2012)

country comparison to the world: 100

**Internet users:**

577,800 (2009)

country comparison to the world: 116

# Chapter 8: Transportation

**Airports:**

> 47 (2013)

> country comparison to the world: 94

**Airports - with paved runways:**

> total: 11

> 2,438 to 3,047 m: 1

> 1,524 to 2,437 m: 3

> 914 to 1,523 m: 6

> under 914 m: 1 (2013)

**Airports - with unpaved runways:**

> total: 36

> 1,524 to 2,437 m: 1

> 914 to 1,523 m: 6

> under 914 m: 29 (2013)

**Railways:**

> total: 59 km

> country comparison to the world: 129

> narrow gauge: 59 km 0.762-m gauge (2008)

**Roadways:**

> total: 10,844 km

> country comparison to the world: 132

> paved: 4,952 km

> unpaved: 5,892 km (2010)

# Chapter 9: Military

**Military branches:**

Nepal Army (2012)

**Military service age and obligation:**

18 years of age for voluntary military service; no
conscription (2014)

**Manpower available for military service:**

males age 16-49: 6,941,152

females age 16-49: 7,618,397 (2010 est.)

**Manpower fit for military service:**

males age 16-49: 5,260,878

females age 16-49: 5,947,512 (2010 est.)

**Manpower reaching militarily significant age annually:**

male: 380,172

female: 367,103 (2010 est.)

**Military expenditures:**

NA% (2012)

1.41% of GDP (2011)

NA% (2010)

# Chapter 10: Transnational Issues

**Disputes - international:**

joint border commission continues to work on contested sections of boundary with India, including the 400 square kilometer dispute over the source of the Kalapani River; India has instituted a stricter border regime to restrict transit of Maoist insurgents and illegal cross-border activities

**Refugees and internationally displaced persons:**

refugees (country of origin): 15,0000-20,000 (Tibet/China) (2012); 29,813 (Bhutan) (2014)

IDPs: 50,000 (remaining from ten-year Maoist insurgency that officially ended in 2006; figure does not include people displaced since 2007 by inter-communal violence and insecurity in the Terai region) (2012)

stateless persons: 800,000 (2011); note - in 2007-2008 the government distributed 2.6 million citizenship certificates to the 3.4 million people without one; the remaining 800,000 without citizenship certificates are not necessarily stateless, and the UNHCR is working with the Nepali Government to clarify their situation; lesser numbers of Bhutanese Hindu refugees of Nepali origin (the Lhotsampa) who were stripped of Bhutanese nationality and forced to flee their country in the late 1980s and early 1990s - and

undocumented Tibetan refugees who arrived in Nepal
prior to the 1990s - are considered stateless

**Illicit drugs:**

illicit producer of cannabis and hashish for the domestic
and international drug markets; transit point for opiates
from Southeast Asia to the West

# Map of Nepal

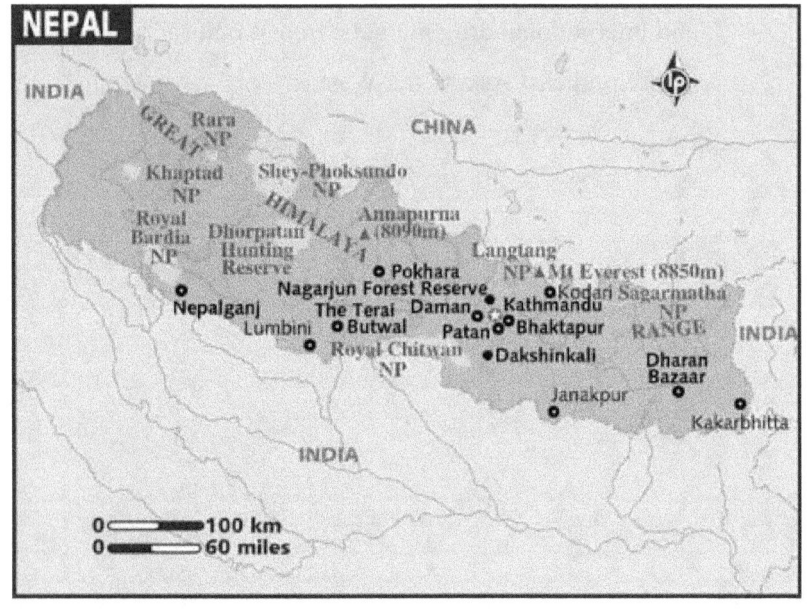

# Other Key Facts™ Titles

Key Facts on South Korea

Key Facts on France

Key Facts on the United Kingdom

Key Facts on Egypt

Key Facts on Israel

All Key Facts™ Titles are Available at

www.Amazon.com

THE INTERNATIONALIST®

2014

WWW.INTERNATIONALIST.COM

www.ingramcontent.com/pod-product-compliance
Lightning Source LLC
Chambersburg PA
CBHW070716180526
45167CB00004B/1498